Loch Ewe

during

World War II

by
Steve Chadwick

1st edition published 1996
Reprinted 2001

Foreword

For some years the Gairloch and District Heritage Society has been anxious that a record be made of the use of Loch Ewe during World War 2. In this the writer of the book has succeeded.

At the commencement of war it became apparent that the existing Naval bases at Rosyth and Invergordon, both situated on the east coast of Scotland, were vulnerable to air attack. After a U-boat penetrated Scapa Flow in Orkney, and sank the Royal Oak in December 1939, that base too was judged unsafe until the defences were strengthened. Accordingly Loch Ewe was selected as an alternative. It was the most northerly of the suitable west coast sea Lochs with the least steaming time to the Atlantic. It had the advantages of being large and well sheltered, of having a relatively narrow entrance, and having a depth suitable for anchoring.

Loch Ewe was used both as a Fleet base and Convoy assembly point. Convoys which braved the appalling journey to north Russia set out from here. At its peak the military personnel well outnumbered local people.

By meticulous research the author has provided a definitive account of all aspects of the history during the six years of war-time activity at Loch Ewe and in the surrounding district. This book will serve not only as the only record of that time, but also as a memorial to the hundreds of seamen who lost their lives on the Russian convoys, for whom the hills around Loch Ewe would be the last sight of land they would ever have.

W. R. M. Murdoch
Chairman
Gairloch and District Heritage Society.
March 1996

Loch Ewe During World War 2

Contents Page

Illustrations

Written by Steve Chadwick.
Published by 'Wilderness Guides'.
Maps by Wendy Price, North Kessock.

ISBN No. 0 9528134 0 8

Preface

To drive past Loch Ewe and Gairloch is to pass through scenery of wild and magnificent proportions. The ribbon of road picks it's tortuous way through cliffs between sea and mountain, with each view seeming to vie with its predecessor for breathtaking grandeur. But what is this that sits ill with the scenery? Rusting metal posts, crumbling concrete edifices, old gun emplacements. What happened here, and why is it thus?

It is with some trepidation that as an amateur historian, I begin to write the World War 2 Loch Ewe story. I began to realise as I researched the area for historical back-ground for my walking guides, that here was history being lost before our eyes. A generation who's memories had to be captured before they were lost for ever. The war saw an almost total black out on pictures and media coverage, and many official records and log books have been lost, so that personal memories are to a large extent all we have to go on.

I have spent many hundreds of pleasant hours making notes and talking with local people and war time personnel who have come back to visit. Indeed Loch Ewe must hold a very special place in many peoples hearts for they come back year after year, but each year fewer return.

Correspondence has come in from all over the world and each piece has helped to fit the jig-saw of a censored history. Some aspects are now fairly well documented, whilst others remain obscured by time and lack of data.

I appeal to anyone who has a story or information on the area during World War II, to let myself or the Gairloch Museum know, and let us record the information before it is lost. If what I say here is wrong or can be added to, let us know!

In writing this I have leant heavily on the actual recorded notes of those involved. I make no apology for this, indeed I feel it adds to the authenticity of the writing to quote directly and to use the style of the originator.

Finally thanks to all those who have given of their time and precious memories. It has been a pleasure during these last eight years to listen to people tell of their past, and to do what I can to bring to light a most remarkable and unsung part of our history.

Steve Chadwick
Gairloch
April 1996.

Royal Naval Presence at Loch Ewe during World War 2

On the 7th of September 1939 the Admiralty gave Admiral Forbes a greatly exaggerated estimate of the bomber strength available in north-west Germany for an attack on Scapa Flow, and ordered a temporary base be prepared on the west coast of Scotland. The Commander-in-Chief selected Loch Ewe and sent the HMS Guardian there to lay anti-submarine nets. For security reasons, until March 1940 Loch Ewe was designated 'Port A'. Between the 9th and 15th September the Fleet flagship and other major units arrived at 'Port A', they included HM ships Nelson, Rodney, Repulse, Ark Royal and Hood. They were visited by the First Sea Lord and returned to Scapa on 21st September, and prolonged discussions on the future of the Fleet's bases began.

On instructions from the Admiralty, Admiral Forbes returned to Loch Ewe on 1st October with the Nelson, Rodney, Hood, Repulse, Ark Royal, and the 6th and 8th Destroyer Flotillas, leaving the Renown and Royal Oak at Scapa Flow. Although, owing to its geographical position, Loch Ewe was less exposed to air attack than Scapa Flow, it was even more unprotected against submarines, for it had only indicator nets and no gate, and was without any shore defences.

When they moved to Loch Ewe, the Royal Oak was left behind at Scapa and insecurity against submarine attack was immediately made apparent. There was now no disguising the danger in which the fleet lay, in its temporary base in Loch Ewe. The Admiralty even considered that it was greater than at Scapa, and agreed to give Loch Ewe priority for certain additional anti-submarine defences. It was certain that before long the Germans would discover that the Home Fleet was using the place as a base. Never-the-less, it was decided that the fleet should remain there for the time being, and Loch Ewe was given priority over Scapa Flow for the provision of guard loops and controlled mines.

The Admiralty were still apprehensive and proposed that the main fleet base should be moved to the Clyde. Admiral Forbes totally disagreed, on the grounds that a whole day would be required to get the fleet into the northern part of the North Sea. He expressed a preference for Rosyth, where the anti-submarine defences were good, and although it was more exposed to air attack, this was offset by better air defences. It was eventually decided that the fleet should remain at sea as much as possible and return alternately to Loch Ewe and the Clyde until the improvements to Scapa had been completed.

At a meeting at the Admiralty on 24th October, the whole question of fleet bases was re-discussed, and it was decided that the Clyde should be used as the main base for the fleet and that Loch Ewe should be abandoned. This decision was signalled to the Commander-in-Chief but Admiral Forbes was still unable to agree. The outcome of a further meeting on the 31st October was finally that Scapa Flow should be the Home Fleet's permanent base, and Loch Ewe would be retained for occasional use. The temporary base for the Fleet at Loch Ewe was by no means ideal for at 07:52 hrs on 4th December as HMS Nelson was entering the Loch she exploded a magnetic mine.

The next phase of Loch Ewe Naval activity centred around its use as a refuelling base for escorts, thereby enabling a new convoy cycle to be introduced from January 1941. Loch Ewe was established as a subsidiary assembly port for convoys, and in view of its growing importance, the naval base was commissioned as HMS Helicon at Aultbea on 14th June 1941. In addition to coastal and Atlantic shipping, convoys for Russia also used Loch Ewe from February 1942. All returned to Loch Ewe, with parts of the later convoys being despatched for the Clyde.

In order to save manpower, on the 14th December 1944 it was proposed to close Loch Ewe as a convoy assembly port in favour of the Clyde. It ceased to operate as such on the 7th January 1945. HMS Helicon continued to operate until the 6th August 1945 when it was paid off.

H.M.S. Nelson at Loch Ewe. Courtesy of Times Newspapers.

Converted Minesweeping Trawler, the Walwyns Castle. Based at Loch Ewe 1945/46. Drawn by Frank Bentley.

The Mining of H.M.S. Nelson
Loch Ewe. December 4th 1939

1922 To 26th October 1939.
The Nelson and the Rodney were designed and built by Armstrong Whitworth at Newcastle-upon-Tyne as part of the 1922-23 Naval building programme. These ships were originally designed in 1921 to have a displacement of 48,000 tons and a top speed of 32 knots, but the Washington conference of 1922 restricted capital ships to 35,000 tons, and as such both ships emerged from the shipyards much restricted in length and beam, and with engines only capable of producing 23 knots at full speed. They retained their originally planned complement of nine - 16" guns but the change in ships dimensions caused the gun turrets and super-structure to look ugly and ungainly, all forecastle with a towering bridge structure called officially '*The Octopoidal*' but was soon nicknamed '*Queen Anne's Mansions*'.

The Nelson's overall dimensions in feet were 710 x 106, with a full draught of about 32 feet. She carried a main armament of nine 16" guns in three turrets, secondary armament was twelve 6" guns. She also carried up to 30 anti aircraft guns including multi barrel weapons, and two 24.5" torpedo tubes. Her engines were rated to 43,000 hp, and as stated produced a maximum speed of 23 knots. Ships complement varied between 1300 and 1360 officers and men. She joined the fleet on Trafalgar Day, 21st October 1927.

At the outbreak of the Second World War, H.M.S. Nelson was attached to the Home Fleet based at Scapa Flow, flying the flag of the Commander-in Chief Admiral Sir Charles Forbes. She soon received a taste of action when on the 26th September she was escorting home the British submarine Spearfish which had been damaged in action off Norway. The Nelson was attacked by German aircraft but escaped without damage.

Between the 9th and the 15th of September the Fleet Flagship the Nelson, accompanied by the Rodney, Repulse, Ark Royal and the Hood, arrived for the first time in Loch Ewe which for security reasons was designated 'Port A' until June 1941. They were visited by Winston Churchill accompanied by the First Sea Lord Sir Dudley Pound, then returned to Scapa on the 21st of September.

On instructions from the Admiralty, Admiral Forbes on board the Nelson returned to Port 'A' on the 1st of October, along with the Rodney, Hood, Repulse, Ark Royal and the 6th Destroyer Flotillas, leaving the Renown, Royal Oak and the cruisers at Scapa Flow. Those instructions would prove fatal for the Royal Oak.

There followed a period of disagreement over where the fleet should be based, but the audacious raid on October 14th by a U-Boat commanded by Gunther Priem resulting in the sinking of the Royal Oak made it clear that Scapa was not ready to act as the base for the home fleet until better defences could be prepared.

For the next few weeks the home fleet was spread between the Clyde, Loch Ewe and Rosyth, though the latter's security became less credible when on the21st November 1939 H.M.S. Belfast was seriously damaged by contacting a magnetic mine about 400 yds east of the Forth Rail Bridge. The mine had been laid by U-21 under the command of Lieutenant Fritz and was one of the first incidences of loss to this new weapon. On the 13th November the destroyer Blanche was sunk by a mine close to the Tounge lighthouse in the Thames estuary, and on the 21st November the destroyer Gipsy was sunk off Harwich.

In late November the armed merchant cruiser Rawalpindi was overwhelmed and sunk by the German battle cruisers Gneisenau and Scharnhorst and the cruisers Koln and Leipzig. A battle group commanded by Admiral Sir Charles Forbes in the Nelson, along with the Rodney, a cruiser and seven destroyers sailed from the Clyde to intercept the German force but were too late as the German ships had escaped to Wilhelmshaven under cover of bad weather. The British force split into two groups and the Nelson with a destroyer escort turned south. On passage the destroyers required fuel and the Commander-in-Chief decided to top them up from the base tanker in Loch Ewe.

Hit by Torpedoes

During this early stage of the war the German navy was having problems with torpedo's that failed to detonate on impact, and it is in this context that the following German naval account makes interesting reading and adds another twist to the story.

Lieutenant Wilhelm Zahn's U-56 was one of the Type 2 coastal vessels built for operations in the North Sea and the Baltic. At 10:00 hrs on the 30th October 1939 the little submarine found itself west of the Orkneys and right in the middle of a powerful contingent of the British Home Fleet. The battleship Rodney had passed out of range but the Nelson was coming into perfect firing position. "Range 800m.......Target 60 degrees......Speed of target 12 knots.......Depth setting 8 meters....... Percussion fuse ready.....**Fire Fire Fire**".

After the torpedo's release the U-56 rose to put her periscope briefly above the water, then hurriedly dived. The Petty Officer held the stop watch in his hand, counting the seconds. Zahn himself put on the ear-phones of the listening apparatus. Suddenly, above the noise of the thrashing battleships propellers they both heard the metallic clang of steel against steel. Others in the crew heard it too, but after the strike - nothing. Then came a second fainter clang with no explosion, after which the noise of the fleet died away.

By now a series of dark cylinders were lying on the sea bed of Loch Ewe and this time the German Navy would have a second and more successful attack on H.M.S. Nelson.

The Mining

On the night of the 27th October 1939, U-31 commanded by Lieut. Johannes Habekost, laid 18 magnetic mines across the entrance to Loch Ewe.

The original intention was for the Nelson to remain waiting off Loch Ewe whilst the escort re-fuelled, but because of reports of enemy submarine activity in the Minch area, Admiral Forbes decided that the Nelson would be better protected from attack inside the arms of the Loch.

At 07:52 hrs on the 4th December 1939 as she was making 13 knots on her way into Loch Ewe, the Nelson detonated one of the mines about 7.3 cables from the north-eastern extremity of Uamh an Tuill, in 19 fathoms of water.

Lieut. Commander A.W.A. Stevens (retired) was on board at the time and relates: "I was part of the Forecastle Division, a member of 10 mess. We had stood down from the Morning Watch of Anti-Aircraft Stations and were ordered to join the Starboard Watch of the cable party on the Fo'csle. On the way for'ard I went down to the messdeck where A.B. Luxton, the messdeck dodger (cleaner) was having a shave using an open razor. Suddenly I found myself being bounced and shaken, together with aluminium messdeck lockers, ditty boxes and attaché cases. The air was thick with cork particles from the fan trunking and deckheads, and after I had climbed out from beneath a pile of lockers I obeyed my first instincts and made for the upper deck. On the ladders were a large number of men with the same idea including one man who was being assisted as his leg was broken.

"On deck we automatically mustered at our emergency stations and I found myself next to the messdeck dodger who gave me my only laugh of the day. He being a cockney said '*Ere Steve, I fort I'd cut me bleedin 'ed orf*'. The ship was sinking slowly at the bows and I amongst others was eyeing the distance to shore in case we had to swim".

Len Corben was a young Royal Marine and part of the cable locker party - " There was a blinding blue flash and all the lights went out. I was thrown heavily, but fortunately away from the bins (which contained the huge anchor chains) and badly damaged my shoulder".

Geoffry Brook was a Midshipman who was having a bath in the communal Gunroom bathroom - "There was an almighty **CRUMP** and my bath leapt about a foot, almost throwing me out. The ship continued to shake in a series of minor convulsions that coincided with an ominous rumbling sound".

Local people remember the explosion well. It was one of those events when you can recall what you were doing at the time.

Up on the bridge, tension was running high. First thoughts were that the ship had been hit by a torpedo and that another could be expected at any moment. The ship took a list of 3 degrees and sank at the bows by 7 feet, but continued to steer perfectly. The Admiral had considered beaching the ship but Captain Miles refused. The Nelson finally anchored at 12:10 after delays due to damage to cables holders and to cruisers being foul of the preferred berth.

The damage was considerable, the mine had blown a very large hole just above the starboard side of the keel and the ship had developed a serious leak causing flooding in stations 16 to 80. The torpedo armament was immobilised and forward 'A' turret was out of alignment and remained so for the rest of the ships life. No boilers, engines, electrical, steering or power machinery were effected, but her fighting efficiency was severely impaired. Portable pumps finally brought the leaking under control by 14:20 hrs on the 5th Dec.

Lieut. Commander Stevens continues: "No one was killed but between 70 to 80 were casualties, some of the injuries were horrific. At that time of day the for'ard heads (toilets) were busy and the occupants had been tossed around several times into the air descending each time onto the sharp jagged edges of broken ceramic toilet pans. One lad who was recovered from the Side Party's Locker looked as if he was bleeding to death but was just completely disorientated and covered with red lead paint.

"The first action was to inform the Admiralty and because we could not break radio silence, Paymaster Midshipman Roy Quinton was sent ashore to telegraph the message from Aultbea Post Office. He had a slight skirmish with the elderly Post Mistress (Alice Cameron), who took some convincing of the urgency of the situation, but he eventually got through".

Secrecy and Repairs

The priorities now became repairs, protection and secrecy, with the latter two being bound closely together. It was very important to keep from the German High Command the news that one of their magnetic mines had succeeded in crippling the Flagship of the home fleet. The army supplied AA guns onshore and long range fighter cover was arranged from the east coast. Two ships the Calcutta and the Cairo were rushed to Loch Ewe to provide further anti-aircraft cover.

George Hunt was a member of the crew of H.M.S. Calcutta: "We had put into Chatham and the first party of Port Watch were sent on 48 hours leave, but two hours later we sailed north at full speed on a mystery run. We sailed up the east coast, through the Pentland Firth and down the west coast of Scotland, arriving at Loch Ewe at 15:00 hrs on Tuesday 5th of December. 'Abandon Ship Stations' was sounded before we entered the Loch, which we did very slowly, and we later found out that a special Prayer Service had been held for us in H.M.S. Nelson".

Besides the Nelson there were five C and D class cruisers of the Northern Patrol in Loch Ewe and all were effectively trapped until mine sweeping measures could be taken. Sweeping with 'M' sweep and coil were organised as soon as possible. Mine sweepers, four drifters, towed skids with huge magnetic coils, and even a Wellington bomber fitted with a coil were all employed in an effort to free the approaches from mines.

On 7th December the Flag of the C-in-C Home Fleet was transferred from H.M.S. Nelson to H.M.S. Warspite which was anchored in the Clyde.

Meanwhile temporary repairs were being effected by the ships crew. Lieut. Commander Stevens again: "The ship's divers using standard suits, i.e. big brass helmets etc. measured the hole. From these dimensions the ships artisans produced an enormous curved tailored patch which was carefully lowered into position and secured with hooked screw bolts. To this day I still marvel at the craftsmanship and expertise of these tradesmen. Christmas came, a traditional one with turkey, plum pudding and all the trimmings, and the last real one I was to experience for many years".

Another sailor was not so fortunate with the festivities. John Campbell was on H.M.S. Belfast when she was in Loch Ewe on 14th October 1939, and was on the same ship a few weeks later when on the 21st of November she set off a magnetic mine near the Forth Road Bridge. He was returned to barracks at Portsmouth, but a few days before Christmas he and other young sailors were told to make ready to move out, destination unknown: "As we kept going northwards by rail towards Perth it was apparent that our destination was Loch Ewe. The end of the line was Achnasheen and after having been on the train for over 24 hours we were bundled into trucks and buses and I was able to tell my companions that we were definitely bound for Loch Ewe.

"The Loch was an impressive sight that evening in late December 1939. There was a full moon and the Aurora Borealis was at it's most impressive. Among the ships at anchor, the silhouette of H.M.S. Nelson with her extended Foc'sle was easily recognisable. We boarded the ship as the Bosun's Calls were sounding 'Pipe Down', so the time must have been 22:00 hrs on the 23rd Dec 39. I was asked if we had our Christmas dinner, and on replying that I had not I was told I wouldn't get any that year as Christmas had been celebrated early as it had been thought that the ship would be sailing through the partially cleared minefield on Christmas day".

During the weeks following the mining, a further five mines were detonated by sweeping operations, and it was not until the 4th January 1940 that is was considered safe enough for the Nelson to sail out of Loch Ewe to Portsmouth for repairs. She left in the care of 6 destroyers, arriving on the 8th January having been delayed by fog.

The departure from Loch Ewe is described by Lieut. Commander Stevens: "We weighed anchor and moved slowly past Isle Ewe with most of the ships company fallen in on the upper deck and only essential personnel below. Off Sgeir Araig a captured German merchant ship was waiting. Manned by volunteers and flooded right down she took station ahead of the Nelson and led the way out and clear of the Loch".

H.M.S. Nelson was out of commission for 7 months until repair work was finally completed at the Clyde on 6th June 1940.

H.M.S. Nelson in Dry Dock, showing mine damage. (PRO reference ADM 267/58)

U-Boat 31

The paths of U-31 and HMS Nelson were inextricably linked during that fateful October in 1939, so it may be of interest if we look a little closer at this U-boat and its eventual fate.

U-31 was a type V11A submarine built by A.G. Weser of Bremen, commissioned in December 1936. German submariners quickly built a reputation for skill and daring, we may not like what they did but it is hard not to feel a pang of admiration for the nerve required to penetrate Scapa Flow. It was against the background of such an exploit that Johannes Habekost took his submarine into the hostile waters of the Minch in late October 1939.

Her ordinance load of torpedoes was reduced on this trip for she also carried 18 magnetic mines to be released from her torpedo tubes. A more correct term is T.M.B. or 'influence mines'. They had a cylindrical shell of aluminium alloy which was said to lay badly on the sea bed. The charge varied from 420 to 560 kg. and the mines were normally laid in 22 to 27 metres of water.

It is believed that the Germans knew of the use of Loch Ewe as an alternative anchorage for the British Fleet, and that their 'Horchdienst' or 'Y' Intelligence, had broken Admiralty codes. U-31 was despatched to lay mines across the entrance to the Loch.

Lieut. Habekost negotiated the Minch and lay off Loch Ewe until dark, then on the evening of the 27th October 1939 he began stealthily edging forward. At periscope depth calling quiet monotone commands he brought his submarine into Loch Ewe, but the German did not know that an anti U-Boat net had been laid across the entrance to the Loch. It was a simple one layer affair with an open gate, meant to be a temporary measure to last until the full three layered net could be put in place. Had the Lieut. known this he could have laid his deadly cargo right around Isle Ewe, but as it was he nosed into the boom and the metal net screeched and scraped on the outer hull. Adrenaline pumped and pulse rates soared but there were no ships nearby to hear the noise and U-31 reversed away from the net undetected.

Unable to penetrate deeply into the Loch, the mines were laid in a line across the entrance roughly from Cove to Leacan Donna. U-Boat records give the position as AM 3826, but this would equate to a position further out in the Minch and we know from the resulting damage to H.M.S. Nelson and subsequent mine sweeping operations, that the mines were laid in the entrance to the Loch itself.

As we know, on the morning of 4th December 1939 H.M.S. Nelson detonated one of the mines laid by U-31. In early 1940 another U-Boat tried to penetrate the Loch Ewe anchorage, but this time the submarine nosed into the three layered boom. This set off a chain of phosphorous flares mounted on the net buoys and anti U-Boat measures were put into immediate effect. Depth charges were fired along the Loch entrance but many were set to explode at too great a depth, so sunk to the sea bed without detonating.

U-31 was sunk by bombs at Jadabused, at 5330N, 0812E, at 1200 hrs on the 11th March 1940. All 58 of the crew were killed including Habekost. The U-Boat was later raised by the Germans, repaired and returned to service. Her new commander was Prelleberg who achieved doubtful success by sinking the 81 ton trawler 'Union Jack' 100 miles north west of the Butt of Lewis on the 22nd Sep 1940, and was credited with finally sinking the 5389 ton ship 'Matina' which had been previously damaged by U-28 a few days earlier.

On the 2nd Nov 1940 U-31 was sunk for the second and final time at 5626N, 1018W by bombs and finally depth charges from the destroyer HMS Antelope. This time only two of the U-31's crew were lost, the survivors being picked up by the Antelope.

Security

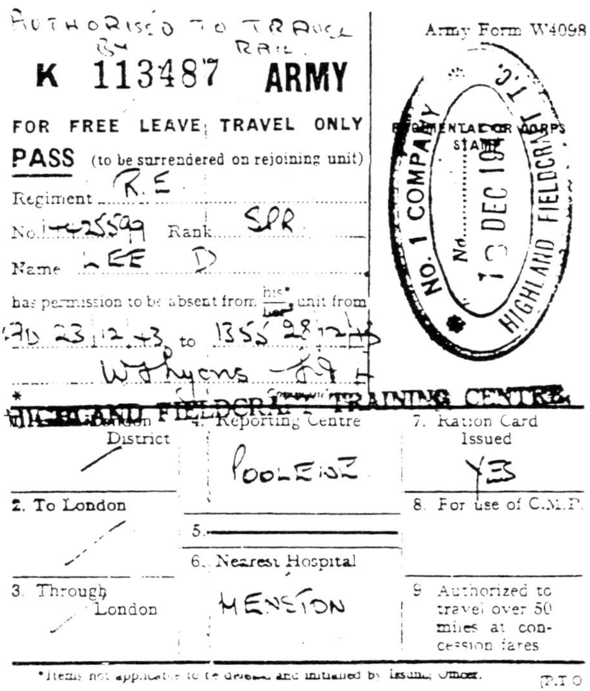

AUTHORISED TO TRAVEL BY RAIL.

Army Form W4098

K 113487 ARMY

FOR FREE LEAVE TRAVEL ONLY

PASS (to be surrendered on rejoining unit)

Regiment R.E.

No. 1425599 Rank SPR

Name LEE D

has permission to be absent from his* unit from

1710 23.12.43 to 1355 28.12.43

HIGHLAND FIELDCRAFT TRAINING CENTRE

1. District	4. Reporting Centre	7. Ration Card Issued YES
2. To London	5.	8. For use of C.M.P.
3. Through London	6. Nearest Hospital MENSTON	9. Authorized to travel over 50 miles at concession fares

*Items not applicable to be deleted and initialled by issuing Officer.

P.T.O

No. 1 COMPANY HIGHLAND FIELDCRAFT T.C.

The whole area around Loch Ewe and Gairloch was a restricted area for the duration of the war. All local people had to carry special passes.

There were several check points where papers would be examined, the first of which was at Inverness Railway Station. At this point all persons on trains going on to Achnasheen were subject to careful checking. At the end of 1940 a further barrier was erected at Achnasheen. The hut that was used still exists, a red corrugated iron hut by the road side near the phone box.

There were two further barriers near Loch Ewe itself, one being by the present Laide Stores, to check all persons coming from the north, and the second, which was for a time in the charge of a Lieut. Turnbull, was by the present Wild Cat Stores in Gairloch. The locals would regularly by-pass the Gairloch check point by walking down by the shore footpath known as the 'low road'. What remains of the Gairloch barrier is stored at the Gairloch Heritage Museum.

Towards the head of Glen Docherty the debris of large concrete blocks with square grooves cut in the sides lie discarded just down the slope. Originally there was a block on each side of the road and three iron bars extended between them. The culvert beneath the road was also mined so that it could be detonated if required. There were as many as eight mined culverts in the area

Home Guard

As with every other part of Britain, the area had it's own Home Guard contingent. With so much military activity in the area their work was very important. Their rifle target practice range was at Gairloch Golf club, and the 'Old Rec (Recreation) Hall', which was their base, is still there at the bottom of the hill from Gairloch School.

By all accounts one of the leaders of the local Guard was a man of some character. He rode a push bike with a fitting on it's handle bars that would take a machine gun. He was also convinced that the Germans would invade at Scoraig and many exercises were based on that scenario.

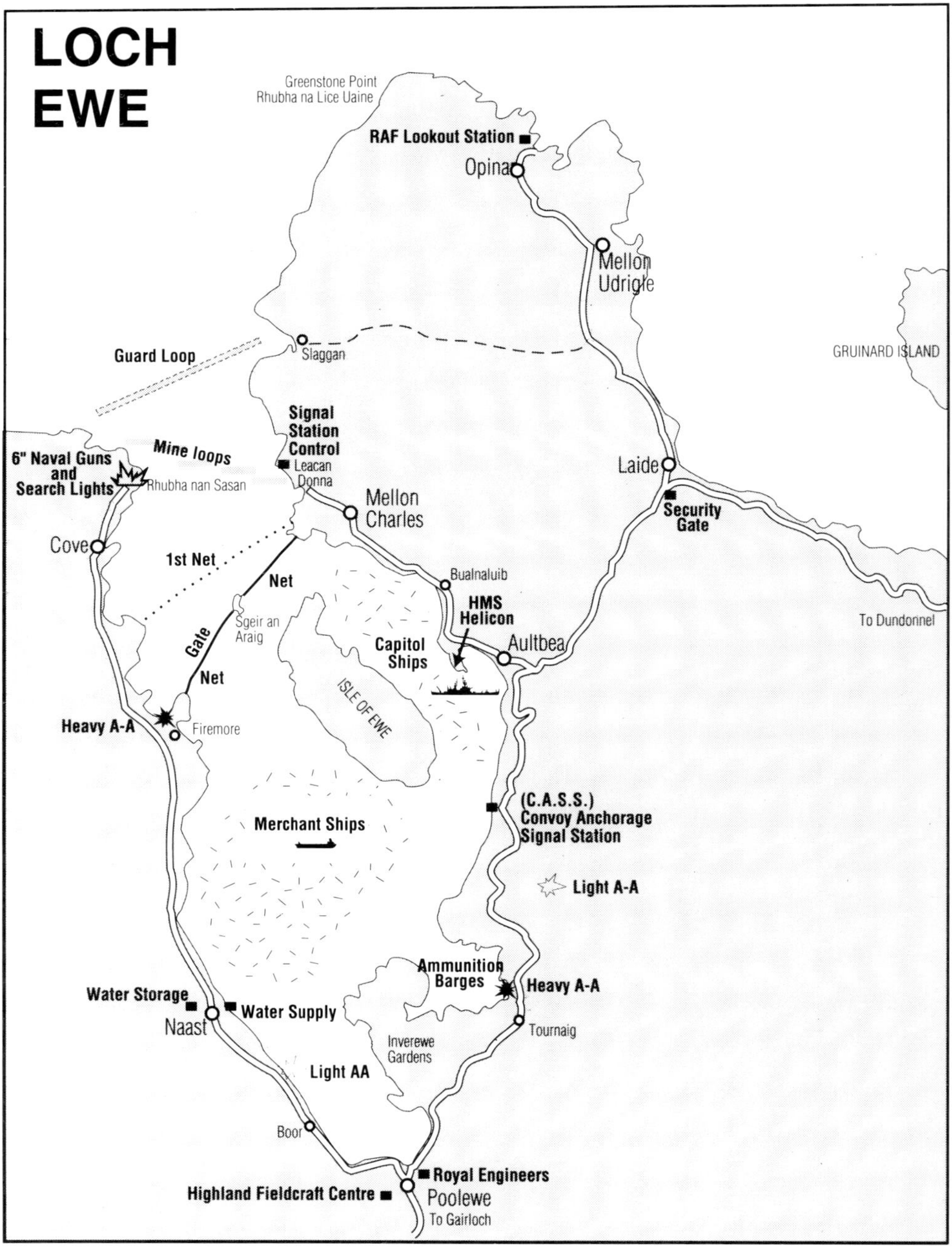
LOCH
EWE
Greenstone Point
Rhubha na Lice Uaine
RAF Lookout Station
Opina
Mellon
Udrigle
GRUINARD ISLAND
Guard Loop
Slaggan
Signal
Station
Control
Leacan
Donna
Mine loops
6" Naval Guns
and
Search Lights
Rhubha nan Sasan
Laide
Security
Gate
Mellon
Charles
Cove
1st Net
Net
Bualnaluib
HMS
Helicon
To Dundonnel
Sgeir an
Araig
Gate
Net
Capitol
Ships
Aultbea
ISLE OF EWE
Heavy A-A
Firemore
(C.A.S.S.)
Convoy Anchorage
Signal Station
Merchant Ships
Light A-A
Ammunition
Barges
Heavy A-A
Water Storage
Water Supply
Naast
Tournaig
Inverewe
Gardens
Light AA
Boor
Royal Engineers
Highland Fieldcraft Centre
Poolewe
To Gairloch

Loch Ewe - The Defences

The dispatching of HMS Guardian to Loch Ewe in September 1939 was the first manifestation of many defensive measures that were to follow as the war progressed. The Guardian laid an anti-submarine net across the mouth of the Loch just to the north of the rocky island of Sgair an Araig. It was a one layer affair with an open gap to act as entry and exit point. For all its simplicity and faults it was enough to deter Lieut. Habekost from entering the inner sanctuary of Loch Ewe in U-boat 31.

The mining of HMS Nelson on December 4th 1939 led to the first anti-aircraft units being rushed to 'Port A' (Loch Ewe). Mr H MacDonald of Inverness recalls "The 297th of the 101 H.A.A. Regt. R.A.T.A. was ordered to travel west immediately. Headquarters were set up in Tournaig House, and 'A' troop with two guns were billeted in the loft above the byre at Tournaig Farm. This was an unwitting master stroke, for the heat rising from the cows below was as good as central heating. The guns were set up across the road but when it came to digging holes for the creation of foundations, they immediately filled with water. Snow fell to a depth of seven inches, much to the distaste of those on guard duty, as all they had was a bell tent and a paraffin stove. Other guns were sited at Mellon Charles from where they could see the badly listing battleship. They were billeted in the Drill Hall at Aultbea and got used to shaving and washing in a mountain burn after breaking the ice. A permanent daylight flight was arranged by the RAF to patrol the sky above the Nelson, dropping identification flares on their approach".

Anti-aircraft

As the importance of Loch Ewe grew, so the temporary AA sites began to be replaced by permanent positions. Light AA guns were positioned on small concrete bases on sites of good elevation around the Loch. Heavy AA sites were positioned at Aultbea, Firemore, and Tournaig which was also anti-aircraft Battery Headquarters. HAA Regimental Headquarters was at Poolewe.

The following is an extract from a 'War Cabinet Chiefs of Staff Committee' and is marked '**Secret**'.

> The existing scale of A/A defences at Loch Ewe are 8 Heavy and 4 Light guns. This is to cover the following functions for the port:-
>
> 1/ As a fuelling and minor storing base for H.M. Ships of the North Western Approaches Escort Force.
>
> 2/ As a transit anchorage for ocean-going merchant vessels bound to, or coming from the east coast.
>
> It is now considered that the importance of Loch Ewe as a convoy anchorage and base has increased to an extent to justify a higher scale of A/A defence. Some 200,000 tons of shipping now use the harbour daily.
>
> Signed: Admiralty S.W.1.
> 12th June 1942

Coastal defence

Rubha nan Sasan beyond Cove was the site of coastal defence artillery. Its fire power came from two six inch guns salvaged from the H.M.S. Iron Duke which had been bombed and beached at Scapa Flow on 17th October 1939. Normally there was one heavy anti-aircraft battery and one troop from a light anti-aircraft battery at Loch Ewe, about 12 officers and 380 men altogether. 379 Battery of 101 Heavy Anti-Aircraft Regiment had the longest stay, from 1941 to April 1942.

Barrage balloons

Balloon Command 990 Squadron was deployed to Loch Ewe on the 24th September 1941. The headquarters of this unit was at Tournaig and the building erected on the foreshore for the purpose of inflating the balloons has recently been renovated for farming use. At one time there were upwards of fifty balloons in the sky above and around the Loch, land and ship bases, with four on Isle Ewe. So many balloons were lost in storms that a reward was posted for their return. At a time of severe rationing of food and materials they made very good hayrick covers, and even ended up as hand bags and purses. Storm losses proved so costly that the use of balloons was eventually discontinued.

Mines and anti-submarine boom

As the base gained in importance sea defences were also improved. Besides the 6" guns at Rubha nan Sasan, a 'guard loop' was placed on the sea bed at the extreme outer limit of the anchorage. It ran from the island of Eilean Furadh Mor in the west to Slaggan Bay in the east. This system detected vessel movements by changes in the electrical field. A series of mines were also deployed on the sea bed from Rubha nan Sasan to the control centre at Leacan Donna, from where they could be detonated if required. A second and far more effective anti-submarine net was also deployed across the Loch. It ran from the rocky point of Rubh a Choin near Mellon Charles, to the Island of Sgeir an Araig, then across to An Sguiteach near Firemore. This was a three layered affair with flares positioned on its surface buoys which would be set off if an attempt to penetrate the net was made. There was a gate controlled by two trawlers, one of which would open two of the layers, whilst the second positioned on the other side of the gate would pull aside the third layer. The theory was that if either vessel was sunk there would still be a layer of the net intact.

The Highland Fieldcraft Training Centre

The Cadet Officers of No. 1 Company

proudly Present their

Third Terrific Revusical

"I CAN HARDLY WAIT"

the Show with Two Famous Forerunners

Produced by Ken Johnstone

Under the patronage and by permission of

LT.-COL. LORD ROWALLAN, M.C., T.D.

in aid of Y.M.C.A. and UNIT FUNDS

THIRTY-SIX MUSICAL FEATURES IN TWENTY-SIX ROUSING SCENES

Garrison Theatre, Poolewe

Friday, 21st January, 1944

at 7-30 p.m.

"Legs" Quantrill

and his

"GREMLINS"

Some Song Numbers, as in "Never a Dull Moment," written by Ralph Reader.

Seats: Forces 6d, 9d, 1/6, Civilians & Officers 1/-, 1/6, 3/6

Programme—Minimum TWOPENCE

Beer Jam Jars

Loch Ewe and Gairloch was a restricted military area in a time of war, but like all established camps, there were light hearted moments. Loch Maree Hotel was used as an R&R (rest and recuperation) centre for Naval officers on convoy duty. The bar of the Aultbea Hotel was always a popular place. The only trouble was that due to war shortages there were no beer glasses, so men bought jam jars or large empty sweet jars. Fred Jarman (the name is entirely coincidental) remembers: "We solved the problem of beer glasses by buying an empty sweet jar from the little shop with the rusty tin roof. The lady at the bar would fill the jar which held just six pints, and the three of us would sit on the beach taking turns to drink it empty. I don't recall how many times we emptied it".

Films and Concerts

Mrs Myra Hook was a WREN who came to the base in October 1941: "One of the wooden huts was the YMCA staffed by a wonderful group of local ladies. This same hut was used for the cinema on Wednesday and Saturday evenings. Once a fortnight there would be a dance with the Base, Naval ships afloat and the Merchant Navy taking it in turns to attend. Dances were on Friday nights and on Saturday mornings there was usually to be seen a rating carrying a pane of glass to replace one broken at the dance. We would have a camp concert now and again and it was surprising how much talent could be mustered, or ordered, for these occasions. These concerts, sometimes ENSA, would also be in the YMCA".

The Highland Fieldcraft Centre had a number of shows at the Poolewe NAAFI. John Trimmer writes: "Legs Quantrill was a platoon commander/instructor who played the saxophone. He formed a band called 'Legs' Quantrill and his Gremlins. We played at officers' dances which gave us a chance to chat up local talent, until the officers moved in!"

Frank Bently, a seaman gunner on board the mine-sweeping trawler 'Walwyns Castle' recalls: "The flotilla boasted a dance band which was much in demand in and around Aultbea and at the Gairloch Hospital. I played the accordion and soon learnt the Scots way of dancing. The band played in halls and schools on the inner and outer Isles as well as the mainland. On VE night the band were paid to stay sober, and the entire base went to town.... There was a German beer garden and coloured lights everywhere."

Loch Ewe to Russia
The Arctic Convoys

The older people of Aultbea talk of the time when their loch was black with ships and it was as if you could walk across the Loch from one side to the other, moving from ship to ship. The vessels were gathering for that most feared of convoys, the Arctic run to Russia.

The Convoys

Laden ships came round from the east coast of Britain, from the Clyde and from America to gather in the anchorage of Loch Ewe, protected as it was by 6" naval guns at Cove to discourage and challenge surface raiders, by heavy and light anti-aircraft guns and by a boom net and mine defence system.

The first Arctic convoys gathered and sailed not from Loch Ewe but from Hvalfjord or Reykjavik in Iceland. Only two of the nineteen 'PQ' series convoys, lasting from 21-Aug-41 to 2-Sep-42 sailed from Loch Ewe. The earlier convoys fared well, suffering little attrition right up to the sailing of PQ-13. Thus far one hundred and thirteen ships had left for Russia and only two had failed to make it. One ship had turned back with engine failure and one from the convoy PQ-7 had been sunk by a U-boat. Convoy PQ-11 was the first to leave direct from Loch Ewe bound for Russia. It left on 6-Feb-42 and duly arrived in Murmansk seventeen days later. It was realised that this good run was unlikely to last for lengthening days would make the ships easier to find, as the forthcoming convoys would find to their cost.

PQ-13 lost five vessels, two being sunk by U-boats, two by aircraft, and a further ship was lost to a German surface raider operating out of Norway. PQ-14 was a disaster due to weather and ice floes. The order to scatter was given and only seven ships got through, though sixteen managed to return to Iceland. PQ-15 and 16 suffered increasing rates of loss culminating in the tragedy of PQ-17 when out of 36 ships that left Reykjavik, only 11 reached Archangel. Two had turned back to Iceland but 13 were sunk by aircraft and a further 10 by U-boats. This rate of attrition was appalling and convoys were suspended until shorter days and protective night could lower down its icy darkness and offer some protection from the marauders.

PQ-18 consisting of forty merchant ships was the first in a series of eighteen convoys that left Loch Ewe for northern Russia, and included the USS 'Patrick Henry', which was the first of 2,770 'Liberty Ships'. The convoy sailed from Loch Ewe on the 2nd Sep 1942.

The nights were getting longer and the Arctic pack ice had yet to begin it's winter march south, which allowed convoys to sail north of Bear Island and thus keep further away from attack by aircraft from German occupied Norway. The route lay north west, through the Denmark Strait, between Iceland and Greenland, where it was protected by escort ships from Western Approaches Command. Once through the Strait the convoy would turn east and hug the pack ice in order to keep as far away from Norway as possible. On the 7th September the convoys long range escort relieved the Western Approaches group, and two days later Admiral Burnett joined with the *Scylla, Avenger*, and half the 'fighting destroyer escort'.

Off Spitzbergen two ships were lost to U -boats. Later forty four Heinkel He 111 torpedo-bombers attacked "*like a huge flight of nightmare locusts*" and sank eight ships for the loss of only five aircraft. The US ammunition ship Mary Luckenbach was hit and disintegrated in a huge explosion. A steward who was outside carrying a cup of coffee to the bridge, was blown half a mile down the convoy, he was the only survivor. The attacks continued until ten ships had gone down to aircraft and three to U-boats. Admiral Burnett considered whether to go on or return home with what ships he had left. He opened his Bible at random to Isaiah chapter 43 and read *"When thou passest through the waters I will be with thee, and through the rivers, they shall not overflow thee. When thou walkest through fire thou shall not be burned. For I am the Lord thy God"*. The convoy went on and lost no more ships, to reach Archangel on the 17th of September 1942.

Loch Ewe Stories

Loch Ewe was growing in importance and had been commissioned as H.M.S. Helicon on 14th June 1941. A wooden hut outside the Aultbea Hotel was base for the first naval contingent of four men who arrived in late 1939. They were Captain Maund, Sub Lieut. Grieve, Signalman Boyes and Writer Bibbings. This was a fortuitous posting for Boyes as he met his future wife Peggy in the hotel where she was working as a cook. This was the first of several marriages resulting from war time postings to the area.

Local people played an important part in the life of the naval base acting as NAAFI workers and helpers of many kinds. Ian Mackenzie of Second Coast worked on the 'DEMS' (defensively equipped merchant ship). These vessels supplied the ships in transit with munitions and other essential supplies. Ian's boat was an old 'Puffer' called the *George Fredrick Brown*, not surprisingly shortened to '*GFB*'. She was in the charge of Captain Roberts, a Cornishman.

A Canadian ship was due to leave for Russia in the next convoy but was short of ammunition for it's Bofors anti-aircraft guns, so on a winter's day of driving rain and high winds Roddy Forbes and John Alec Mackenzie drove two lorries across the moors on the single track road to Inverness. There they loaded up with munitions and started back. The storm was raging with violent gusts of wind plucking at the vehicles, and heavy rain making visibility very difficult. Finally one lorry went into a ditch at Dundonnell. The remaining lorry went on to Aultbea to off load it's cargo and the came back to it's stranded twin. In the height of the storm Roddy, John and other helpers laboured to transfer the live shells and then drove back to Aultbea. At Loch Ewe Captain Roberts was waiting for the final load, and once on board the *GFB* set off through the stormy seas to find the Canadian ship. A destroyer had also stayed behind to escort the merchant ship, and once the munitions were on board both ships set off at full speed to catch up with the convoy.

Captain Roberts was 'Officially recognised' for his work in bringing the shells through the storm to the waiting ship. No doubt very deserved, but I can't help thinking that the two drivers of that day also did valiant work.

Recently Captain James Coleman USN, USMM (Ret'd) wrote to the people of Aultbea to tell of his experiences one New Years Eve, whilst waiting for his convoy to sail for Russia. I quote direct from his narrative. "A lady Sub-Lieutenant came up and said "*Captain, would you like to attend a dance and New Years Eve party*". I enquired if I could bring anything , she replied "*oh no, but if you have a bit of spirits*". I told her I had a couple of bottles of scotch that I could contribute.

"We finally arrived at the decorated village hall to find the band already playing. One old woman asked "*are you from the colonies*", I could only smile and said 'I am from America'. She then said "*that is what I asked you*". I had to change the subject rather quickly. It was quite a party. They danced to bagpipe music as well, and that was a sight to behold. I was not that nimble but what the hell, I tried anyway. The band began to play Auld Lang Syne and all the people began to sing. I sang in English but many were singing in Gaelic. When they came to one part of the song they shook hands and lifted their drinks to each other, this happened several times.

"With tearful good-byes we filed aboard the bus to take us to Loch Ewe. You could feel the glow of the wonderful time we had all experienced. As the bus got underway I noticed there was not a cloud in the sky and a full moon. I could see the hills so clearly, bathed in moonlight. One of the group started singing a Scottish song and then everyone joined in. This was sort of a crowning glory for me on this trip, the wonderful company, the party, the dancing, the beautiful moonlight in the highlands, and now these youngsters singing the songs of their ancestors. The wonderful feeling was a welcome for me for I would soon be sailing into harms way. Some of us would never return".

One story begins with Mrs Sawyer of Inverewe House, the daughter of Osgood Mackenzie. A relation of Marie Sawyer, Admiral Sir Angus Cunningham-Graham, was to join a Cruiser Squadron detailed to protect a convoy bound for Murmansk. After an evening meal together, Mrs Sawyer gave her cousin six Rhododendron plants which were duly taken on board ship and survived the voyage to Russia. On arrival in Murmansk the Admiral's Flag Lieutenant told him that one of his Squadron Captains wished to see him. This was the Captain of H.M.S. Rhododendron, who had heard of the travelling bushes. A present was made of one to the Captain. This plant survived the war and now flourishes in Sussex. It is believed the remaining five grow in retirement near Dumbarton.

Finale

Loch Ewe continued to host the gathering of ships bound for the Arctic route until the last convoy sailed on the 30th December 1944. Altogether four hundred and eighty one merchant ships and over one hundred naval escort vessels left Loch Ewe for Russia in a total of nineteen convoys. For many hundreds of men who made the ultimate sacrifice, the cold grey water of the North Atlantic is their resting place. For these men the enfolding arms of Loch Ewe and the outer isles fading in the distance was the last sight of land they had, before the Russian convoys exacted their terrible price paid in human lives.

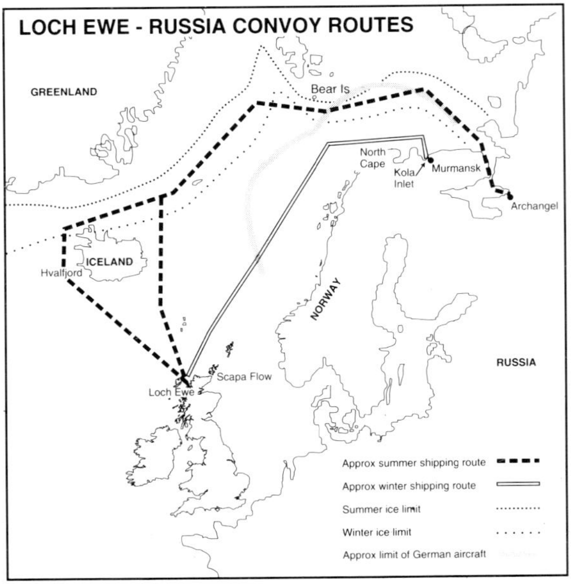

Statistics of Loch Ewe Outbound Arctic Convoys

Convoy	Date of sailing	Number Sailed	Number of Merchant Ships Lost	Royal Naval Actions
PQ-11	6-Feb-42	13	0	
PQ-18	21-May-42	40	10 by aircraft 3 by U-boat	
JW-51A	15-Dec-42	16	0	
JW-51B	22-Dec-42	14	0	*Achates & Bramble* sunk. German destroyer *Eckholdt* sunk.
JW-52	17-Jan-43	14	0	
JW-53	15-Feb-43	28	0	
JW-54A	15-Nov-43	18	0	
JW-54B	22-Nov-43	14	0	
JW-55A	12-Dec-43	19	0	
JW-55B	20-Dec-43	19	0	*Scharnhorst* sunk.
JW-56A	12-Jan-43	20	3 by U-boat	
JW-56B	22-Jan-43	16	0	*Hardy* sunk by U-boat.
JW-57	20-Feb-44	42	0	*Mahtatta* sunk by U-boat.
JW-58	27-Mar-44	49	0	
JW-59	15-Aug-44	33	0	*Kite* sunk by U-boat.
JW-60	19-Sep-44	30	0	
JW-61	20-Oct-44	39	0	
JW-62	29-Nov-44	30	0	
JW-63	30-Dec-44	35	0	

Returning convoys also had to run the gauntlet of German attacks, and there was also no rest whilst at anchor in Russia as a German air base was only 50 miles away.

Altogether merchant shipping losses were over 100 and over 800 men lost their lives.

Naval losses were 2 Cruisers, 7 Destroyers, 7 Sloops-Frigates and Corvettes, 4 Minesweepers, 1 Armed Whaler, and 1 Submarine sunk by 'friendly fire'.

German Naval losses were 1 Battlecruiser, 4 'other' surfce warships, and over 30 U-boats.

The Anchorage

Once ships had passed the examination vessel and were through the boom net they were allocated places to anchor. Only the convoy commodore's ship was allowed to moor up to a buoy, which gave direct communications with CASS (Convoy Anchorage Signal Station). The concrete base of CASS may still be seen on a high point of the road just south of the current NATO refuelling pier.

The merchant shipping anchorage was south and west of Isle Ewe, whilst Royal Navy vessels were always anchored between the island and Aultbea. Loch Thurnaig was reserved for barges and any vessels carrying munitions. These for obvious reasons were kept well away from other ships.

The Base

Rodney and Peggy Stokoe describe the R.N. Base: " On entering the gateway to the base there were few buildings on the waters edge left hand side of the road. There was first the shipwrights workshop, a parking place for two large 'desert' ambulances, the NAAFI (Navy, Army & Airforce Institute), various marine equipment stores, then the road curved to the jetty on the end of which was a wharf with a small shed and a crane.

"On the right of the same roadway, after passing the guardhouse, which also contained the jail, there was a long shed housing the electrical workshops, then a cul-de-sac leading to the chapel, after which was the NAAFI for the "lower deck" personnel. Then the road branches past the pay office, the naval clothing store, the Captain's house overlooking the jetty, a rum store, then the wardroom or officers' quarters. Back to the right turn after the NAAFI, one passed through a complex containing living quarters for the 'crew'. Turning left brought one to the sick bay followed by an uphill left turn to the W.R.E.N"s quarters".

The first unit to be posted to Loch Ewe consisted of four men, Captain Maund, Sub Lieut. Grieves, Signalman Boyes, and Writer Bibbings. They were based in a wooden hut by the side of the Aultbea Hotel. Alan Stenning arrived in January 1940 and recalls the base: "I was a young signalman when Loch Ewe was hastily opened up as a fleet anchorage. Port 'A', as it was called, turned out to be a *secret naval base* somewhere on the wild west coast of Scotland, so secret in fact that the British traitor Lord Haw Haw from time to time referred to it in his broadcasts from Germany, saying that his masters knew all about it and which ships were hiding there! The postal address was *Port 'A', C/O GPO, London*, so our families discovered from Lord Haw Haw where we were based. An embryo base was already in being, under the command of Captain L.E.H. Maund. The Captain and his officers lived and 'messed' in the Aultbea Hotel, whilst I was billeted in the Forbes croft. Two others were billeted on the village policeman!"

"Hitherto the offices consisted of a long wooden hut divided into small sections. The 'signal station' was an Aldis lamp flashed from the window! Contractors moved in and started to erect new base buildings adjacent to Aultbea pier. By June 1940 the buildings were complete and occupation started, the largest contained the various offices. There were several long huts for rating's messes, dormitories, and kitchens etc. the 'Wrennery' was situated at a discreet distance away.

"In early June 1940 the first contingent of WRENs arrived to the joy of all concerned. They acted as office staff, telephonists, stewards, cooks, and teleprinter operators. I married one of the latter two years later.

"The sailors and WRENs would watch eagerly for the bus, carrying the mail, coming down the hillside in the evening. There was little to do in off watch periods except walk and swim if you were tough enough.

"A small signal station and lookout point was established at Leacan Donna. This was manned by half a dozen seamen. We did a weeks duty rota at Leacan Donna, and it was always a pleasant respite from normal routine. Later in the year a controlled minefield was established, together with a permanent staff so our 'weeks holiday' came to and end.

"My wife and I returned recently, and stood looking at the derelict buildings of Leacan Donna. A flood of memories came back, though it was sad to see how much history has been allowed to decay."

Convoy anchored in Loch Ewe. Beinn Airigh Charr in the background. National Maritime Museum (N 38553)

The Staffordshire in Loch Ewe. After bombing whilst returning from Russia. National Maritime Museum (N 37519)

Loch Ewe Air Raids

Accurate information regarding attacks by aircraft is difficult to obtain. Official records show four raids during June 1941, and there is no doubt that this was the busiest period, but it would seem that there were at least seven raids on Loch Ewe. To make matters worse German records do not always correspond with records from Loch Ewe. Some military personnel talk of many reconnaissance visits by high flying German planes, which would be additional to actual attacks.

To some extent human error accounts for lack of records. The raids that were detected in time for anti-aircraft measures to be taken are quite well documented, whilst the surprise attacks that went undetected until too late are hardly mentioned. No one wants to talk too much about how they were caught out.

Officially Recorded Air Raids

June 7th 1941

Warning received 01:07 hrs. At 01:15 E3 (AA unit at Tournaig) fired one round and E1 (AA unit at Rubh a Choin) fired four rounds at a JU-88 dive bombed the anchorage.

At 01:25, E1 fired two rounds and then another two at 01:38 hrs, and finally four rounds of shrapnel. The last appeared to burst close to the aircraft which at once fired all its guns at the site without causing casualties or damage.

At 01:45 hrs E3 fired two rounds. Two bombs near missed *H.M.S. Ethiopian* (the store ship) causing external damage. One plane acted as decoy for the second aircraft which followed with its engines cut out, and dropped two bombs.

June 8th 1941

Warning received at 00:05 hrs. 01:10 hrs aircraft engines heard to S of E1. Plane travelling S to N at point just south of E1, identified as JU-88. Four rounds fired and aircraft departed northwards at 35,000 ft.

Another JU-88 observed from E1 just over surface of Loch and engaged with one round from No. 2 gun.

01:30 hrs. Plane observed to N flying at 4000 ft. E1 fired three rounds, burst close to target.

01:35 hrs. E3 fired two rounds of shrapnel at aircraft which dived at anchorage from the south. Three further rounds fires at second aircraft flying at 4000 ft, using open sights until predictor got on target, when another three rounds were fired. Two other aircraft followed and E3 fired four rounds of shrapnel.

June 21st 1941

17:02 hrs. Six JU-88s sighted. E1 fired one round, E3 fired three, height was within 10,500 ft. No hostile act reported.

June 24th 1941.

15:03 hrs. E3 engaged JU-88 which made landfall over Greenstone Point at 15,000 ft. Six rounds fired. Raider climbed to 25,000 ft and doubled back northwards.

The above engagements were by AA units established on well made concrete bases. The first AA units were brought over from Inverness to protect H.M.S. Nelson after she had detonated the magnetic mine.

Junkers JU-88A-4

The Trawler Michael Griffith Opens fire

Charlie Jones was on board the minesweeping trawler *Michael Griffith* which was based for a short time at Loch Ewe in June 1941, he writes: "The air raid sirens went about 01:00, we all jumped to Action Stations. Our armament was a 12-pounder and two Lewis guns. We saw three or four German bombers fly over the Loch from the East to begin their bombing run, and the Captain gave the order to **Open Fire!** The 12 pounder loosed it's first round and the charge exploded close to one of the planes, then to the crew's anger and disbelief the gun jammed. The ship's main armament was now out of action but the men on the Lewis guns kept firing. The red tracer reached upwards into the sky whilst the white tracer of the planes raked the land and sea. One tracer run came straight for our ship and the top sides men ducked for cover until they realised they had sheltered behind a sheet of canvas! The bullets passed by and no one was hurt. On shore by Cove people saw one plane leave a trail of smoke as it lost height flying out towards the Minch. The next morning we went to sweep the channel to the Loch and found an empty orange rubber dingy with German markings".

A German Account of the June 7th Air Raid

We have on record the report of the German pilot who led that raid, and it makes interesting reading to view events from the 'other side'. Their base was at Stavanger, Norway.

"6th June 1941. Stoffregen calls me to the command post. I am to lead a formation of five aircraft to attack a gathering of ships discovered on the west coast of Scotland, the place is called Loch Ewe. I am proud when I call together the crew allotted to me. I know them, and with the exception of Scheller all have had some operational experience. We take off at 22:00 hrs, fly at low level over the sea, reach the critical 'sneak through' point between the Orkneys and the Shetlands, and continue westwards before turning south towards Cape Wrath. From there we climb slowly over land towards our target. It is long past midnight but still light when we recognise Loch Ewe from 30km distant. Tension mounts as we get nearer the target and begin to distinguish details of the inlet. Each pilot selects his own target except Scheller who scurries on ahead at full throttle and spoils our surprise totally. Now we receive a veritable hail of AA fire and there is no chance of carrying out a successful attack by diving into that red wall of tracer fire.

Whilst the others are diving and drawing fire on themselves, Hans and I detect a particularly large ship in the middle of the bay, that belongs to us! I level off and dive on it without bothering about my dive brakes. When the 'fat pot' is clearly in my sight, I press the bomb release button. I pull back on the control column with all my might while the dark cliffs grow higher into the sky. For God's sake don't let us smash into the water now! We finally manage to level off just above the waves. Theo shouts something on the intercom whilst we climb steeply into the pale sky, "Peter, man - we have hit it! It is an enormous ship".

We simplify our return flight by whizzing low along the famous Loch Ness, and are the last to land at Stavanger. We report one big ship badly damaged".

Many points of the German account tally with what we know from our own records and from eye witnesses. It seems that the 'big pot' that received the bombs was in fact the small island of Sgeir an Araig, which lies just north east of Isle Ewe. It is boat shaped, and as it was the centre mooring point for the boom net across the loch entrance, it had a number of buildings and masts along its length, thus in the heat of the moment could easily have been mistaken for a large vessel.

Unexploded Bomb
In the late eighties a scallop diver found a large cylindrical object on the sea bed just north of Sgeir an Araig. It is believed to be what remains of a large anti ship bomb dropped by the German plane on June 7th 1941. It is still there, illegal trawl nets beware!

Local People Remember
Kate Macleay recalls the cheeky single plane that made a mid-day attack by coming in at very low level over Greenstone Point. She and her school friends were out in the Balnaluib school play ground during lunch break when the JU-88 came in. It was banking round and was so low that the German pilot waved to the children as he passed over. Meanwhile the Headmaster was going apopleptic, shouting to get the children back inside. Lexi Trotter was working in the Aultbea Hotel and hid in a corridor, bomb detonations caused ceiling plaster to come down on her head. Jessie McIvor was walking along the roadside and hid in a culvert beneath the road.

Doctor Hunter was at Talladale attending the birth of Donny McKay's brother. He saw the gun fire and flashes, and thought Aultbea was being wiped out.

One bomb is reported to have landed in Gairloch, and a faulty anti aircraft shell fell and exploded at the top of the Lonemore road.

Air Raid Damage
In the final event damage from air raids was slight. The base supply ship H.M.S. Ethiopia received near a miss and suffered minor damage. A merchant ship, the Devon, received a near miss that broke her back and she had to be beached. An oiler vessel was transferring fuel to a Cruiser just off Aird Point. A bomb missed but its fin flew off and cut though the fuel line and there was a considerable oil spill.

German Losses
On June 7th 1941 combined anti aircraft fire did bring down one JU-88. A story that has a lot of credibility locally is that a vessel manned by Norwegians was first to find the survivors in an inflatable dingy floating in the Minch. There was little love between

Germans and Norwegians in those days, and the story goes that the Germans were dispatched to the bottom of the sea.

Charlie Jones was onboard the mine sweeping trawler Michael Griffith when later that morning they came across the empty orange inflatable dingy.

Ann Munro was convalescing from appendicitis at Laide when she was woken by gunfire. She watched the tracer fire above Aultbea and was startled by a German plane coming low over Laide with obvious engine trouble. It disappeared out to sea over the Minch.

German records show one plane returning from a raid over Loch Ewe sent out a distress call saying he was going down near the Shetlands.

The next noted German aircraft loss in the area was not recorded at Loch Ewe as a raid or reconnaissance flight, and indeed it may be that its reason for being in the area had nothing to do with Loch Ewe.

The Scoraig Affair

A Junkers JU-188D-3 from Aufklarugsgruppe 1(F) 120, reconnaissance unit, based in Norway, crashed in Little Loch Broom at about 18:15 hrs on Dec 28th 1944. It seems likely that all four of the crew managed to escape prior to ditching though only flight engineer Unteroffizer Heinz Josef was lucky enough to make a parachute descent to land a few metres from the edge of Little Loch Broom. The other three are presumed to have died at sea, the body of W. Neugebauer (OBS) was washed up at Camas Mor on December 29th. A further body presumed to be Offz. H. Koestner was found at Duncanna on February 15th 1945.

Heinz Josef had landed at an unknown place in the middle of winter, and did what most would do; he headed for the nearest lighted window. At home on the remote Scoraig peninsular in the only house for many miles was Mrs Joey Stewart, then a teenage girl, her sister and Mother. "There on the doorstep stood this tall figure speaking a foreign language and putting his hands above his head. When I saw this I reached out for the revolver he had in his hand, and I beckoned him in. We gave him food and dry clothes, then I went to the nearest neighbour to ask him to inform the authorities. He in turn had to cross the loch to reach the nearest telephone. The German knew several languages but no English so I tried Latin that I had learnt at school. He had also learnt Latin at school so we conversed using Latin and sign language. Within a few hours some officers and an armed guard sailed into the loch on a Naval boat, but could not return with the prisoner immediately as a storm blew up".

A local related to me of how the boat trip from Loch Ewe to Scoraig and back was so rough that the Loch Ewe policeman who made the trip swore he would never go to sea again.

Medical Support

The military in the area had two locations of medical assistance. The Gairloch Hospital (Hotel) was used early in the war by the R.A.M.C. and later taken over by the Navy. The second was the medical unit based at Loch Ewe.

Loch Ewe

Mr R Stokoe who now lives in Canada writes: "Following a period of twelve months intensive training at the Royal Naval Hospital at Plymouth, I qualified as a Naval Sick Berth Attendant and received my first posting, it was to HMS Helicon, which I thought was a war ship! I was directed to proceed to Inverness, then to get on the Kyle of Lochalsh train but to get off at the hitherto unheard-of place called Achnasheen. I arrived in the early twilight to be greeted by softly falling rain (some things never change). I loaded my kit onto a brown three-ton army lorry, and after passing through the guarded gate across the road, we set off through magnificent highland scenery. No information as to our destination was forthcoming from our driver, a dour Gaelic speaking highlander. It was a complete surprise when, surmounting the crest of yet another hill, I found myself gazing down at a huge sea-loch crowded with ships of every kind. I was to become the fourth member of the sick bay staff, presided over by two Surgeon-Lieutenants. Up until the time that the Gairloch Hotel Hospital was taken over by the Navy, the base was served by Hospital ships which were converted cross channel steamers, they were the St Julian, St Andrew, or the St David.

"If a vessel came in flying a white flag with a blue border and a red rectangle in the centre, or she was flashing the letter 'W', we knew she required medical assistance. We would respond to calls for help in a Buckie herring drifter called the 'Craig Alvah' which was our floating ambulance and dispensary. On one occasion following some strong refreshment given by a grateful ship's Captain, one of our doctors missed his footing while attempting to climb down the ladder, narrowly missed the Craig Alvah, and splashed ingloriously into 'the drink'!

"Most of the eventual eight hundred men and two hundred women stationed at Loch Ewe came from large cities and found the isolation quite stressful. There was a saying that went 'when you've been here six months you start talking to yourself; when you've been here twelve months you start talking to the sheep; and when you've been here eighteen months the sheep start talking to you!

"Needless to say, the arrival of the Wrens alleviated the stress, and not a few romances began. One of the ambulance drivers from the base was Peggy, and within six months we were engaged."

Gairloch Hospital

The Gairloch Hotel had been requisitioned for use as a Hospital initially by the Royal Army Medical Corps. It was turned over to the Navy in 1942-3, and the Loch Ewe Hospital ship was withdrawn.

Eileen Downes was a Wren posted to Gairloch Hospital as a driver. Like all military personnel posted to the area, she arrived via Achnasheen. "The mail bus was awaiting its passengers, and we began the journey to Aultbea. There had been a few groans from the naval ratings who were dismayed at the isolation of the area, but happiness prevailed aided to a large extent by the warm and friendly attitude of the local population. One of our favourite pastimes was to go with the local keeper Gordon McNicol, up to the Mill Loch above the hospital, where Gordon would teach us to fly fish. Later the Laird, a Mackenzie, was taken ill and was operated on at the hospital. He was so grateful that he gave us leave to fish his lochs. I did not like to tell him we had been fishing them for months!"

This is a copy of the 1943 original oil painting (using regular ship's paints) done by Jim Paterson, Mate, of the Craig Alvah, a Scottish Herring Drifter converted to War use as a floating ambulance and dispensary servicing the convoy vessels anchored in Loch Ewe. A red, white and blue flag (visible just above the funnel) was flown by the ship on the right, indicating "I need medical help" — a message usually confirmed in Morse code flash lamp (Aldis) to the Signal Station on the hill at the south end of the Loch.

The Base and Local People

There were times during the war when military personnel outnumbered the local population by 3 to 1, so there was scope for considerable friction, but this never occurred. At the October 1939 review of capital ships in Loch Ewe, Winston Churchill was onboard HMS Nelson. He sent out a message to all ships personnel that: "This is a God Fearing community, and every person should behave whilst ashore".

However, in the best of organisations accidents will occur. Mr T. Evans writes from Plymouth. "In 1942 we were on a Colony Class Cruiser H.M.S. Bermuda, and were on speed trials when we put in to Loch Ewe for a weekend break. I was asleep off-watch when about 14:00 hrs I was awoken by a terrific bang, and thinking we had been 'tin fished' (hit by a torpedo) I rushed up the ladder to the upper deck. It was there that I heard that one of the lads had invited some A.T.S. girls from a shore base, to show them round, and when asked by a L/Corporal '*How do you fire the AA guns*' the guide had pulled the lanyard and hey presto one big bang! The shell went about two miles and landed in a farm yard, killed a sow and some piglets, and knocked a baby out of its pram. A delegation off the ship went to the farm to apologise, the baby was not hurt".

The only known infraction was when several chickens were '*requisitioned*' from a hen house on the Isle Ewe. Apart from marriages between servicemen and WRENS, there were also several marriages between servicemen and local girls. Signalman Boyes was one of the first four naval personnel to arrive at Aultbea. He met and married Peggy McLennan who was working as a cook at the Aultbea Hotel.

Bella Marae had reason to thank the Military Hospital at Gairloch, when she began having pains and ended up having her appendix out. Every person from the services that I speak with has only good memories of local people, who generally took them to their hearts, and in many cases into their homes as servicmen were billeted on them.

Local people also played an important role in helping at the base, Kate Macleay worked at the post office run by the formidible Alice Cameron, and would deal with between 80 and 250 telegrams and cables every day. They worked in the various NAAFI's along the coast, and crewed the various support vessels. Much important work was carried out willingly by local people without which the overall effort would have been much harder to achieve.

The Highland Fieldcraft Training Centre
Poolewe

The setting up of this unit should be remembered not only for the work it achieved in the training of future army officers but also for laying down foundations of the Outward Bound Schools that were to follow.

At the end of May 1941 the newly appointed Adjutant General Sir Ronald Forbes Adams was becoming increasingly concerned with the failure rate of men and women being selected for commissions. "We had the problem of young men whom the Board reported as potential leaders but immature. At first these men were returned to their units for further training, but the general reaction of an R.S.M. to a man whom he knew he would lose was to put him in the cookhouse! In January 1943 I asked Dr. Kurt Hahn (of Gordonstoun School fame) to come and see me, and as a result of this I asked Major General Sir John Whitaker - Director of Military Training - whether he would set up some form of 'Outward Bound' training centres. An ex-Canadian timber camp near Glenfeshie was found and even more important he produced Lord Rowallan.

1943 - Lord Rowallan
"I received a telegram on the 24th April telling me to report at once to the Director of Military Training and be prepared to travel to Scotland that night. I was told of the concern at the number of young fellows appearing before the War Office Selection Boards graded N.Y. (Not Yet) and who after a period of military training had made no progress, did I think that a period of concentrated scouting would be of value? I said I was sure it would"!

Glen Feshie and Poolewe
By May 1943 12 officers and 24 sergeants assembled at No 1 camp Glen Feshie, which they took over from the Mountain and Snow Warfare Training Centre. In winter Glen Feshie sometimes became impassable so by the winter of 1943 Poolewe had been chosen as the ideal coastal base with it's mix of sea and mountains.

Lord Rowallan comments: "The whole course was designed to re-cultivate the senses which had become atrophied in modern civilisation....to fill your minds with new ideas and to show you a vision of wider interests to keep you alert and to stimulate your imagination. The exhausting marches were not only to make you fit in mind and body, but to also teach you that there was always a little extra available however exhausted you might be".

The period that followed turned out to be an important part of the lives of the young men who passed through the centre, and formed an integral part of the back cloth that was Poolewe in the second world war. In particular a great loyalty sprung up between the trainees and Lord Rowallan.

Grenade Fishing
One story is told by Roy Wallace about another officer trainee W.G. Marshall, who decided to 'fish' the river Ewe. "Some Canadian lumberjacks had told Marshall of an easy way to catch salmon by dropping hand grenades into the river. The idea appealed to him and as he had a thunderflash left over he decided to see if it would work as well as a grenade. He took two friends to where he knew salmon usually lurked and after some ceremony, dropped the thunderflash into the water. The explosion was terrific and water

cascaded over a large area. Before it had subsided there was a bellow from across the other side of the river and a familiar voice demanded to know who had let off that explosion. They were confronted by a very angry Lord Rowallan complete in hunting gear with a deer-stalker and fishing rod! He repeated the question and Marshall confessed. The C.O. then told him to '**come here**' but Marshall was undecided as he couldn't see a bridge anywhere. The next order was '**through the water**"!

Officers went on from Poolewe to serve with distinction in many parts of the world, many unfortunately dying in battle.

The Wreck of the USS William H. Welch

The William H. Welch was one of 2708 so called 'Liberty Ships' built for the US Maritime Commission between 1939 and 1945. She was launched from the Bethlehem-Fairfield shipyard on March 10th 1943. It was the vice-commodore ship of 10 merchantmen which formed Convoy EN50, and was on passage from London via Loch Ewe to assemble with other vessels before going on to New York.

The Wreck

On February 26th 1944 as the convoy was approaching Loch Ewe they had the misfortune to encounter one of the most savage winter storms that local people can ever remember. The William Welch missed her correct entry, was broached by heavy seas and was washed towards the south western shore by the fierce north easterly storm. She had no cargo and was ballasted down with water but she was difficult to handle and was pushed inexorably towards the mainland just south of the island of Eilean Furadh Mor. At 04:20 hrs she struck a reef just off the tip of the island and stuck fast to be immediately pounded by heavy seas. A British escort tug tried three times to fire a line to the stricken vessel, but all attempts were lost in the maelstrom of the wind and she put about for Aultbea to raise help.

As the ship settled and was gripped more firmly on the grating rocks the Captain ordered all the crew to don their life jackets and retreat to the bridge area which was furthest out of the water. At 06:00 hrs the ship gave up the unequal struggle and broke in two. The bow end was still buoyant and floated away, whilst the crew began to be plucked from the vessel by the huge crashing waves.

The Rescue

Onshore two groups independently came upon the tragedy. Troops from No 6 course of the Highland Fieldcraft Training Centre at Poolewe were on exercises in the area and came upon the scene. Flares that had been fired at around 06:00 hrs were seen despite the weather by Charles McDonald the local Coast Guard, and with companions he set out immediately to find out what was happening.

The sight that met their eyes was devastating. Through the snow storm they could just make out the stranded section of the ship, and were able to see men being washed off the bridge. Some had been washed onto the island and could not be reached, they would shortly die of exposure. Others were being smashed against the rocks on the headlands, whilst bodies and a few lucky survivors had made it onto the shingle beach of Black Bay. Two men made the shore alive and set off for help, by luck they stumbled onto the crofts at Cove and blurted out their story. Immediately three ladies, Jean Mackenzie, Mary McLean and Kirsty McDonald, set off to help, carrying blankets and pots of hot tea.

Duncan Mackenzie and Alex Combe were lighthouse keepers at Rubha Reidh 6 km to the West. Alex Combe remembers: "Duncan and I left the lighthouse about 09:30 hrs. The trip over snow covered peat bogs has nothing to recommend it, but we made good time. We had nearly reached Black Bay when we saw three men approaching us. When we reached them we did what we could to ease their distress, they were without shoes or socks and had been wandering about in the bitterly cold conditions. Rounding the point we found one survivor sitting in a pool of slush and water. He was completely naked and unable to move, so I helped him from the water. We reached Black Bay and helped others search the beach for remaining survivors. They were in a weakened condition owing to exposure and the heavy crude oil almost entirely covered their bodies. Fortunately the navy eventually arrived overland from Cove and soon all the survivors were being attended to round a timber fire which had been gathered and lit by local women who had arrived earlier".

On the beach at Black Bay Charles McDonald, Kenny Gunn and Ken McLean were wading into the savage surf risking their own lives in order to pull luckless seamen ashore. Troops from the Fieldcraft Centre assisted and scoured the cliffs for any bodies. One was spotted at the back of a crevice and two men ran one and a half miles through the snow to Cove for a ladder. One member of the troop jumped across a gap to a rock where a negro survivor was clinging and managed to return ashore with him. The ladies managed to build a fire of driftwood and warmed the tea. As survivors were brought to them they cleaned the oil from their mouths and noses and wrapped them in their hand made precious blankets. Two ladies set off back to Cove carrying a survivor, whilst 70 year old Donald McDonald carried one survivor to Cove on his back.

Rodney Stokoe a medical sick berth attendant at Aultbea recalls: "It was close to 11:00 hrs when the base was first informed of the catastrophe, with an urgent appeal for medical aid. Around ten seamen and two of us boarded a lorry and set off. At Cove the Seamen streamed across the moor leaving Ian and I on the snow covered peat bog without a soul in sight. We struggled painfully over the atrocious surface carrying a stretcher and three blankets. After an age we became aware of surf accompanied by an eerie intermittent clanking noise. We topped the last hill and there before us was the rocky shore; the source of the clanking was now apparent. Two separate halves of a liberty ship were beached on the island and the forepart was rolling from side to side as each fresh onslaught of waves hit it. As it did so the clanking noise rang out from inside it. We saw smoke rising in the air, and as the last of the daylight gave out we arrived at a fire of driftwood around which huddled several men caked in oil. Some of the survivors were groaning and I produced a bottle of whisky - a godsend if there ever was one. An occasional survivor was brought to join us, then to our relief a second rescue party of burly properly equipped men arrived. Back at the road end a lorry was quickly filled with survivors and driven off to the Royal Naval Sick Quarters (Gairloch Hospital)".

One stretcher party member tells: "Darkness was falling and it was a long exhausting time. Once the stretcher fell out of control because of the extremely difficult country and very slippery snow. This journey was a nightmare, with a delirious seaman to carry......he screamed for his wife and mother back home in New Jersey, then fell silent. It took us four hours to reach the road head at Cove, where the waiting doctor pronounced the seaman dead".

As it got dark the local Coast Guard Charles McDonald asked the officer in charge of the army detachment to make one more search, this time back from the beach and cliffs. They found faltering, bloody footsteps in the snow leading to an unconscious seaman. McDonald said, "The lad was nearly done, but he came round. Wasn't I pleased".

Gairloch Hospital
Eileen Downes was one of the WREN drivers who picked up the survivors that day: "At 15:00 hrs we received word that '*there's been a wreck*'. The ambulance started up and together with a nurse we set off. The drive was serious and having arrived at Cove we

could hardly force open the door against the wind to get the stretchers out. In the croft we were aghast at the news of the savage ordeal endured by seamen and rescuers alike since the early hours. The crofters were calm and kind and gave us hot tea. As darkness was falling we returned to Gairloch with two survivors. Then we were told to return to Cove to pick up men from the Highland Fieldcraft Centre who had been in the thick of the rescue and bring them to the hospital. I was told that one of them had been diving off cliffs to reach a victim.

Days later, when the survivors were sufficiently recovered I was sent to Cove to fetch the crofters who had played such a noble part in the rescue. I was a bit surprised at the sight of so many people at the roadside, all holding baskets of gifts, like eggs. They were determined to squeeze in somehow, and happily all was well. When Forbes the S.B.A. on duty saw the group of crofters standing in the doorway of the ward, he called to the survivors sitting on their beds '*Here are the people who saved your lives*', and the men came forward to shake hands".

Out of a crew of 74 only 40 bodies were ever recovered, and of those only 12 survived.

The United States Maritime Service states: "It was the crofters who came to the aid of our merchant seamen on the worst winters night of the year. In a day of snow, hail and biting cold, they carried blankets off their own beds and tea representing weeks of meagre rations, over miles of rocky moors to revive the exhausted men. For hours they searched the boulder strewn beaches for survivors and are credited with saving several lives".

Today the island of Eileen Furadh Mor is a bird sanctuary, whilst its high tide line is still marked by the flotsam wreckage of that day. Onshore at the aptly named Black Bay two rusting lifeboats that the crew were unable to use lie stranded as a forlorn reminder of the tragedy that took place.

U.S.S. William H. Welch by U.S. Coast Guard. By courtesy of the William Hultgren Collection, Pennsylvania, U.S.A.

Gruinard Island

Biological warfare may seem once removed from reality up here in the wild and lovely north west Highlands, and yet an island no more than 1 km from the mainland was the site chosen for a frightening experiment.

It was feared that Germany was developing biological weapons and our own scientists were instructed to find out if such weapons were viable. A microbe had to be found that would withstand being detonated in a bomb, and Gruinard Island was chosen as the site for the experiment.

In the Autumn of 1941 scientists from Porton Down were rowed across to the island, carrying with them a canister of brown soup like liquid. They handled it very carefully, for it was full of 'Bacillus Anthracis', concentrated Anthrax. Sheep and cows were tethered around the site and the team donned airtight suits. Major Allan Younger was attached to the group as an explosives expert. "They asked me to help load the weapon. One of the scientists poured the brown gruel into a container which I held nervously. I had been told just how toxic this stuff was, and knew that if I'd inhaled even the tiniest bit, that would have been it".

An explosive charge was placed next to the container and all personnel withdrew from the island. As soon as an offshore wind blew, the charge was exploded, and the deadly anthrax spores drifted over the animals and out to sea.

The animals began to die a day after the explosion, and within a few days all were dead. More tests were carried out. A Wellington bomber made a low level simulated attack on the island, dropping a small bomb containing more Anthrax. The deadly spores survived the explosion, and again all the animals died. The scientists crossed to the island most days and with them went soldiers, all wearing special suits, to dispose of the dead animals by throwing them over a cliff. They finally covered them up by detonating the cliff and burying the animals under tons of rubble.

The area was alive with rumour as to what was happening on the island. This wasn't helped when a dead sheep floated over to the sands of Mellon Udrigle and infected local sheep. It was buried deep in the sand of the beach, and we presume it is still there. A vet was installed in the Hotel in Aultbea to investigate any further outbreaks.

The result of the Gruinard experiment shocked the scientists. It proved that bacteriological agents of unbelievable toxicity could be harnessed and would be more powerful than any use of gas or conventional weapons. One military expert said: "Just a few ounces would be enough to kill a battalion of 800 men".

From 1947 onwards the island was visited periodically by scientists who took soil samples for analysis. It became clear that Anthrax spores would live in the soil for 100 to 1000 years. In 1971 the spores were about 6" deep in the soil, and shortly after, in order to keep the curious away, the Government erected warning signs ringing the island at 400m intervals.

GRUINARD ISLAND
THIS ISLAND IS GOVERNMENT PROPERTY
THE GROUND IS CONTAMINATED
WITH ANTHRAX AND DANGEROUS
LANDING IS PROHIBITED

All might have quietly continued, the islands yearly check by scientists going on, but in the mid eighties a protest group visited the island, collected a bag of soil and delivered it to the Government. It may be unrelated but in the summer of 1987 the Ministry of Defence spent half a million pounds hiring a contractor to spray and soak the island in a mixture of formaldehyde and sea water.

In February 1990 the Ministry gave the island the all clear, and the island reverted back to the original owners who have reasonably insisted that the MoD supply them with complete indemnity. For the past few years now the island has hosted a number of sheep and many lambs have now been born. It seems fitting that an experiment in death should give way to new life.

Victory in Europe

A local man remembers: "V.E. Day, 8th May 1945, the weather was favourable. The school children went to the peat moor and collected bog fir for a bonfire. Many of the men went to the local hotel for a celebration drink.

"When evening came the crofters windows were once again lit-up and the bonfire was ignited. The ships still in Loch Ewe put up a beautiful rocket display accompanied by the sounding of ships hooters".

H.M.S. Helicon put on a 16 act 'Rousing Revue, rich in Colour and Variety'.

Opinan - Mellon Udrigle - Laide - Aultbea - Mellon Charles

At Opinan, tucked behind the furthest house, on a small rise before the sea is the concrete base of an RAF observation post. Under the sands of Mellon Udrigle lie the remains of the sheep washed up from the Gruinard Anthrax experiment. Gruinard Island itself is visible 4 km to the south east. South from here on the hill to the left called Meall nam Meallan was a civilian observation post. Continuing on past Loch na Beiste is the turning right to Slaggan. For walkers there is the 10 km round trip to the lonely deserted ruins, the bay of which was the eastern extremity of the underwater 'Guard Loop'. Back to the main coast road at Laide, where there was a manned security post with a barrier across the road. South west to Aultbea and take the first turn off to the sea. To the right of the junction bottom lies a garage which is still with the Forbes family as it was during the war. In front of you is the Aultbea Hotel where the first four men of the naval contingent were based in a wooden hut just next to the hotel. Take a jam jar in and ask for a pint, you might need to say you are re-living a war time experience!

Along the sea front to the pier junction. To the right is the original Romney concrete building built during the war as a cinema and social centre. Still in good use by the local people as a community centre. A little dilapidated now on the outside, but should be regarded as a listed building. Just across the road from the Romney building is a well preserved heavy anti aircraft site. To the left is the pier road. This was lined with wooden buildings containing offices, messes, sleeping quarters, etc. a busy place teeming with forces personnel.

North west past Bualnaluib where the German pilot waved to the school children whilst on his lone mid-day bombing mission. On to Mellon Charles and the present day naval base which was the war time boom (anti-submarine net) base. To the left the promontory of Rubh a Choin was the easterly landfall of the boom net. This is on private ground and cannot be reached. Parking is available at the road end from where it is possible to walk the short track to Leacan Donna, which was a signals station and controlled the underwater mine loops. In a inlet to the left (take care) you can still see in place the clamps that held the mine loops control and fixture cables.

Aultbea - Tournaig - Poolewe - Naast - Inverasdale - Cove

Leave the Aultbea Hotel and drive along the sea front to the main coast road. The way twists round 'Z' bends as it gains height. Below to the right is the current NATO re-fuelling pier, whilst to the left on the hillside lie the buried fuel tanks. Look for a high point to the right of the road, it has a concrete base and steps can be made out on its right. This was the site of CASS, the Convoy Anchorage Signal Station. This unit was charged with all convoy communications. Radio was not used in case it was listened to by the enemy, so all signals were by lamp, flags, or by direct phone line link to the convoy commodore's ship, which was moored to a special buoy. The hill side above the road contains concrete bases of light anti-aircraft positions. Past fine view points you come down to Loch Thurnaig where the munitions barges were moored. The water tower built for the heavy anti-aircraft base is still in use, as is the building that was used to supply barrage balloons to ships at anchor. In the field past the water tower lie several heavy anti-aircraft gun positions. The hillside behind the road was the site of the first use of radar in the area.

The road now takes you past Inverewe Gardens, whilst out of sight on the peninsular to the right lie ruins that are something of an enigma. There are two jetties and small concrete bases around the point which we take to be small signal and observation points. But just below the high point of the hill of Ploc an Rubha lie the ruins of a large camp. Can anyone help us trace the history of this site.

Dropping down to Poolewe we pass a modern caravan site on the left. Until 1994 the large concrete bases of a REMY (Engineers) workshops could be seen here. In front of you at the junction is the Scottish Episcopal Church of St Maelrubha. Inside the church is a commemorative plaque in memory of the Highland Fieldcraft Centre, who's camp was behind the church on the site now occupied by a group of modern houses. Take the right turn to pass by Poolewe hotel where an army intelligence unit was billeted, and on out to Boor and Naast. The road rises gradually until 1 km north from Boor you pass on the right what is known as the 'Three Penny Bit', this is a Bofors anti-aircraft gun site. Dropping down to Naast the large (currently) white square looking house was built towards the end of the war as a water pumping station for the bunkering of vessels. The hill and burn on the left carry the ruins of various tanks and weirs.

Through Inverasdale and on to Firemore where there was a heavy anti-aircraft gun site. The old emplacements now shelter caravans and the occasional cow from the elements. A unit from India was based here for a period. They kept their own mules and goats which escaped on occasion, and caused havoc as they were chased by hordes of shouting Indians through the fields of the nearby crofts. The curved roofed building by the Firemore junction was used by this unit, and after the war housed an engineering firm that made tractors for the crofting community.

Drive on past Cove to the road end. Spare a thought for the victims of the William Welch tragedy, and those who went out to help them. A 2 km walk along the shore will take you to Black Bay and the rusting remains of two life boats. The site of Rubha nan Sasan has had to be fenced off due to the increasing derelict condition of the concrete buildings, and the danger they pose to the public. It is possible to walk up the rise to the right to gain a view of the site that held two 6" naval guns, and two coast artillery searchlights.

Poolewe - Gairloch - Loch Maree

The brae up from Poolewe is steep and passes by the view point from where it is possible to gaze the length of lovely Loch Maree. To the left you pass Loch Tollaidh, whilst out of sight 100m on the right are the bases of the old Army camp. The panorama of the Minch and the Isle of Skye open up as you drive down the Auchtercairn brae. By the Wildcat general store at the foot of the brae there was another security post with a barrier across the road. Gairloch Hotel was used as a Hospital first by the Army and then by the Navy. Room three was the operating theatre, whilst room five was the morgue, a point to ponder when booking a room!

Behind the burial ground next to the Church of Scotland are the concrete bases of buildings used by the RASC, Royal Army Service Corps.

Finally the drive through Kerry, down to Slattadale and on to Loch Maree. A fitting end is the lovely setting of Loch Maree Hotel. This was used as 'Rest and Recuperation' for seagoing officers before they faced the uncertain future of convoy duty. For a short period a single barrage balloon was moored here.

Loch Ewe Today

A strange marriage of old and new sometimes makes its presence felt at Loch Ewe. Convoys of military vehicles wend their way along single track roads that their World War 2 predecessors would have recognised. Rapier missiles are set up and their turrets rotate and point from a concrete base that fifty years ago supported anti-aircraft guns that did a similar job. Beyond Cove at Rubha nan Sasan, a complete radar installation appears, and the old NAAFI hut base once more dispenses cups of tea and coffee, though this time from a large tent. Out at sea modern NATO war ships play simulated war games and come into Loch Ewe to refuel. The Hotels bars ring again to voices of servicemen and women, and the Loch takes on a little of the way it must have been many years ago when war was not a game, but a deadly reality.

Sometimes in summer I walk along the headland of Cove at sunset, when the concrete vestiges of war stand stark against the dying sun. It is possible to close your eyes and let your mind see images of many years ago. The roar of a Bedford truck as it disgorges troops, the hum of generators that power guns and searchlights, the slamming of the NAAFI door as a private comes out carrying steaming mugs of tea for those on duty. Out in the Loch a convoy gathers; on board the ships are hundreds of men and each is wondering if this will be his last voyage. At the high point at the back of the Loch the signal station flashes out a message on the Aldis lamp and the convoy weighs anchor. Out in the Minch the destroyers are waiting to shepherd their charges through the icy waters of the North Atlantic. I open my eyes and the echoes fade away, just the gulls are left soaring on the last of the days warm updrafts, before they too disappear to rest for the night.

Index